Happy Holidays!

HAPPY HALLOWEEN!

By Alex Appleby

Gareth Stevens Publishing

Please visit our website, www.garethstevens.com. For a free color catalog of all our high-quality books, call toll free 1-800-542-2595 or fax 1-877-542-2596.

Library of Congress Cataloging-in-Publication Data

Appleby, Alex.
Happy Halloween! / by Alex Appleby.
p. cm. — (Happy holidays!)
Includes index.
ISBN 978-1-4339-9941-3 (pbk.)
ISBN 978-1-4339-9942-0 (6-pack)
ISBN 978-1-4339-9939-0 (library binding)
1. Halloween — Juvenile literature. I. Appleby, Alex. II. Title.
GT4965.A66 2014
394.2—d23

First Edition

Published in 2014 by
Gareth Stevens Publishing
111 East 14th Street, Suite 349
New York, NY 10003

Editor: Ryan Nagelhout
Designer: Sarah Liddell

Photo credits: Cover, p. 1 udra11/Shutterstock.com; pp. 5, 7 © iStockphoto.com/MariaPavlova; p. 9 Ariel Skelley/The Image Bank/Getty Images; p. 11 Brocreative/Shutterstock.com; p. 13 Rob Hainer/Shutterstock.com; p. 15 Hurst Photo/Shutterstock.com; p. 17 kali9/E+/Getty Images; pp. 19, 24 (toys) JeniFoto/Shutterstock.com; pp. 21, 24 (pumpkins) urbanlight/Shutterstock.com; p. 23 Sandra Cunningham/Shutterstock.com.

Printed in the United States of America

CPSIA compliance information: Batch #CW14GS: For further information contact Gareth Stevens, New York, New York at 1-800-542-2595.

Contents

Halloween is
a great holiday.

It happens
on October 31.

People love to dress up.

Some people dress like animals.

Others dress
like people.

Kids go door-to-door dressed up.

People give
them candy.

They sometimes give out toys!

We like
to pick pumpkins.

Some people put faces on them.

Words to Know

pumpkins

toys

Index